ESSENTIAL OILS
Natural Remedies For Your Dog

Safe, Non-Toxic & Frugal Solutions For All Breeds

by Coco Armstrong

CLADD
PUBLISHING

Cladd Publishing Inc.
USA

This publication is designed to provide accurate information regarding the subject matter covered. It is sold with the understanding that neither the author nor the publisher is providing medical, legal or other professional advice or services. Always seek advice from a competent professional before using any of the information in this book. The author and the publisher specifically disclaim any liability that is incurred from the use or application of the contents of this book.

Essential Oils Natural Remedies for Your Dog: Safe, Non-Toxic & Frugal Solutions For All Breeds

ISBN 978-1-946881-28-1 (e-book)
ISBN 978-1-946881-35-9 (paperback)

Contents

Natural Solutions Work Better

When we use store-bought products heavily laced in chemicals, we are destroying our pet's natural ability to heal. In addition to healing the original issue, their bodies now must repair the side effects of the chemicals.

We need be focusing on aiding and boosting our dog's ability to heal themselves. This can easily be achieved by using age-old techniques that are completely safe, non-toxic and have absolutely zero chemicals.

This book is designed using recipes and techniques that utilize essential oils, plant based carrier oils, whole foods and baking soda. You will find all that you need to tackle everyday issues like fleas and ticks, dental, cleaning, stress relief, parasites and cures to common ailments.

Toxins Found in Dog Products

There are so many medications and topical solutions for your doggie. However, most of them will include toxins that will rapidly deteriorate your dog's health.

Deadly ingredients found in top-brand Dog Products:

FIPRONIL

The EPA's Pesticide Division, found that the active ingredient Fipronil (in most top brands) remains in a pet's system with the potential for nervous system and thyroid toxicity.

Laboratory animal test resulted in thyroid cancer and altered thyroid hormones, liver and kidney toxicity, reduced fertility and convulsions.

IMIDACLOPRID

In lab studies Imidacloprid has been found to increase cholesterol levels in dogs, cause thyroid lesions, create liver toxicity. It also has the potential to damage the liver, heart, lungs, spleen, adrenals, brain, and gonads.

This dangerous neurotoxin, can cause incoordination along with labored breathing and muscle weakness. Imidacloprid is readily found in Advantage and other top brands.

When this drug was tested after its introduction in 1994, researchers found an increase in the frequency of birth defects. In the Journal of Pesticide Reform, thyroid lesions are a result of exposure to imidacloprid.

PYRETHRINS

It has been a misconception that Pyrethrins (naturally occurring compounds from the chrysanthemum plant) and pyrethroids (the synthetic counterpart) are less hazardous than other ingredients.

But pyrethroid-based insecticides were actually causing double the fatalities in our dogs than that of other flea treatments without this ingredient. Pyrethroid also accounted for more than half of the "more serious" pesticide reactions including brain damage, heart attacks and seizures.

PERMETHRIN AND/OR PYRIPROXYFEN

Bio Spot Flea and Tick Control, Defend EXspot Treatment and Zodiac FleaTrol Spot On, all contain either or both of the active ingredients Permethrin and/or Pyriproxyfen.

Permethrin is a carcinogenic insecticide. This ingredient causes lung cancer and liver tumors in lab animals. It can also act as a neurotoxin, causing tremors as well as increased aggressive behavior and learning difficulties. This is a substitute ingredient for brands looking to escape the negative publicity of the other more common ingredients.

Essential Oils Q&A

Q: WHAT DOES EO MEAN?

A: EO or EOs is the abbreviation for Essential Oils. It is commonly used and will be used throughout this book.

Q: WILL I BE ABLE TO DO THIS WITH LITTLE EXPERIENCE?

A: This is an excellent book for normal people wanting to enhance their dog's life with Essential Oils, but do not want to spend an erroneous amount of money and time learning techniques from scratch.

Q: CAN I SUBSTITUTE EOs?

A: You can swap out oils or substitute for your favorite in almost all cases.

Q: GLASS BOTTLE OR PLASTIC?

A: Essential oils can degrade plastic. That is way its recommended to store oils in glass.

Q: BASE PRODUCT VS. CARRIER OIL?

A: A base product is a cream, lotion, shampoo, gel or anything that has already been made. You can add a few drops of Essential Oils to enhance the product.

A Carrier Oil is a pure oil, that is used to dilute the strength of EOs, and help prolong its aroma. In addition to carrier oils, many times you will be diluting the oils in water as a spray, bath or soak.

Q: CAN I ADJUST THE STRENGTH OF THE RECIPE?

A: Yes, you can and should limit the drops of EO based on your dog's personal sensitivity towards the strength. Most recipes in this book are light-medium strength. However, you can always reduce or increase slightly in either direction unless stated.

Carrier Oils

The scent of EOs will evaporate quickly, unless combined with a carrier oil. Carrier oils usually come from the fatty portion of a plant and help the essential oils maintain their scent for long periods of time.

Safe Carrier Oils for Dogs

Carrier Oils are important for diluting your EOs prior to ingesting or direct use on your dog's skin.

EXCELLENT CARRIER OILS FOR DOGS:
- Jojoba Oil
- Olive Oil
- Coconut Oil

Supreme Essential Oils for Dogs

LAVENDER OIL

Lavender oil is considered one of the most versatile essential oils. It effortlessly creats a sense of peace and harmony in dogs, and humans. Lavender oil is soothing to the central nervous system. It can ease car ride anxiety and car sickness as well as help with allergies and insomnia.

CEDARWOOD OIL

Cedarwood oil, is known for its powerful ability to repel and kill pests like fleas. It has a wide range of beneficial properties, including being an antiseptic for the lungs. It stimulates circulation and is good for relieving stiffness due to increasing age, arthritis and pulled muscles.

Cedarwood aids in the elimination of dandruff, and strengthens kidney function. It is regularly used as a calming tonic for nervous aggression, extremely shy or timid, or those suffering from severe separation issues.

LEMONGRASS OIL

Lemongrass oil is a well-known insect repellent. It rids fleas, ticks, and mosquitoes, due to its high citral and geraniol content. Your dog's coat will also enjoy the extra dose of nutrients.

How To:

- Add 2-3 drops of the oil to water in a spray bottle, and then apply the spray to your pet's coat and massage through.

CITRONELLA OIL

Citronella oil is also known for its insect-repelling abilities. It is one of the only dog friendly oils that is effective on a species of mosquito known as Aedes Aegypti, whose bite causes Yellow Fever.

How To:

- Add 2 to 3 drops to water in a spray bottle and massaging through your dog's coat.

FRANKINCENSE OIL

Frankincense soothes the nerves and ease anxiety. It has even been used to help cancer, reducing tumors, external ulcers, replenishes and strengthening the immune system.

SPEARMINT OIL

Spearmint oil supports weight loss and aids in diarrhea and colic. It's used to balance metabolism and stimulates the bladder. Spearmint oil is commonly used to reduce gastrointestinal issues in dogs.

CARDAMOM OIL

Cardamom is well-known for its benefits to the digestive and respiratory system. It helps to maintain optimal gastrointestinal balance, ease indigestion and calm stomach upset. Cardamom oil supports respiratory health and promote better breathing. It can uplift the mood of a depressed or anxiety-ridden dog. Diffusing it can help create a calming environment for your pet.

Achy Muscles

If your dog is suffering from aching muscles or general soreness, put them at ease.

HOW TO:

- Mix 3 drops of Copaiba EO
- 2 drops of lavender EO
- 1 tablespoon of jojoba
- Into a small glass jar or roller
- Gently massage into their skin as needed
- Takes 10-20 minutes to start relieving pain

Amber Resin Collars

Baltic amber resin collars are a life saver for flea and tick prevention. It is a wonderful product and is super cute. Amber is a resin that formed millions of years ago. It has electrostatic properties that repels fleas and ticks. Amber also has a light earthy aroma and a beautiful appearance.

Electrostatic electricity makes it impossible for fleas, ticks, and other bugs to remain on your pet's coat. The raw amber has healing qualities for animals as well as humans.

What to look for

The amber must be raw and unpolished. When shopping, look for raw high-quality resin stones, strong collars, and the ability to create your own collar size based on actual neck measurements.

Calming Room Spray

If you have a dog that is displaying anxiety or nervous behaviour, use the Calming Room spray. It will sooth their nerves and help them relax without the use of medications or stress wraps.

HOW TO:

- Add 5 drops of cedarwood EO
- 5 drops of Lavender EO
- Into an 8-oz. spray bottle
- Fill the bottle up to the top with purified water
- Place the spray nozzle on the bottle
- Spray on or around your dog (avoiding face and eyes)

Deodorize Pet Bedding

Eliminate odors from your pets bedding. This is a safe and effective way to deodorize in between washes.

HOW TO:
- Sprinkle baking soda all over your pet's bedding
- Let it sit for 1-24 hours
- Vacuum or shake out well

Sensitive Dog Shampoo

By using a sensitive shampoo on your dog, there will be less irritation on their delicate skin. You will notice less rashes, itching, dandruff, and dark spots.

HOW TO:
- Mix 2 cups of water
- 2 cups aloe Vera
- 4 tablespoons of castile soap
- 4 tablespoons of jojoba oil
- 5 drops of lavender EO
- 2 drops of thieves EO
- 2 drops of roman chamomile EO
- 2 drops of rosemary EO
- 2 drops of lemon or grapefruit EO
- 2 drops of citronella EO
- 1 drop of cedarwood EO
- Pour the contents into a pump bottle
- Use as needed

Dry-Itchy Skin Conditioner

This is a luxurious conditioner specifically for dry-itchy skin that needs extra moisture.

How To:
- Mix 5 drops of lavender EO
- 3 drops of roman chamomile EO
- 3 drops of frankincense EO
- 3 drops of vitamin E
- 2 tablespoons of coconut oil
- Store in a small glass jar
- Use as needed

Ear Health

Use a Q-tip to rub the essential oil mixture in the ear, being careful not to put the Q-tip in past where you can see it- Do this twice a day until you see healthy skin.

How To:
- Combine 5 drops of Lavender
- 5 drops of Melaleuca
- 5 drops of Geranium
- In 1 Tbsp. of coconut oil
- Use a Q-tip to swab the inside of your dog's ear

Flea Bath

Wash your pooch to kill fleas on the spot.

Ingredients:
- 1/2 cup of freshly squeezed lemon juice
- 1 ½ – 2 cups of fresh water
- 1/4 –1/2 cup of shampoo

DIRECTIONS:
Stir together a half a cup of lemon juice, 1 ½ cups of water, and ¼ cup of mild pet shampoo. Bottle the remainder and use every few days until fleas are gone. Make sure that you message the mixture deep into the hair and rinse well.

Flea Deterring Drink

I love using this flea deterring drink for my doggies. They don't mind the vinegar and I feel much better about them running around the yard or playing with other dogs.

Ingredients:
- 1 teaspoon white distilled vinegar or apple cider vinegar
- Purified Water

DIRECTIONS:
For every 5-pound dog add 1/8 teaspoon of white distilled vinegar or apple cider vinegar to ½ cup drinking water. For a pooch that weighs around 10 lbs. double the recipe. I highly recommend using Braggs Apple Cider Vinegar. This solution will improve skin and coat condition from the inside-out.

Know Your Enemy: Fleas

Kill fleas with ease

There are so many wonderful non-toxic remedies that you can use, as well as organic store-bought formulas to fight fleas. As I have mentioned previously the toxins found in common flea and tick medications are deadly to our dogs.

10 Flea Facts:

1. A flea can drink 15 times its weight in blood in just a single day!
2. Scientists have found over 2,000 types of fleas and continue to find different ones each year!
3. The biggest flea that has been found measured in at about 2.5cm!
4. Scientists have shown that fleas can jump up to 8 inches!
5. Fleas have been known to live for two years after having just a single meal of blood!
6. For every flea that you find in your home, there are statistically about 80 others hidden from your sight!
7. Pets with fleas can develop anemia and tapeworms.
8. Research shows that fleas have been around for over 165 million years!
9. Humans can get fleas and suffer from small sores and allergies.
10. Fleas live in moist shaded areas (overgrown bushes or shrubbery)

Flea Spray

This flea spray is an easy way to prevent fleas as well as ticks from hitching a ride on your pooch. It also makes their hair shimmer for days on end.

Ingredients:
- 1 cup apple cider vinegar OR a 50/50 blend of both
- 1-quart fresh water
- 2-3 drops of lavender or cedar oil
- 1 medium/large sized spray bottle

DIRECTIONS:
Add 2-3 drops of oil with 1 cup of apple cider vinegar. Then mix with 1 quart of fresh water. Fill your spray bottle, and mist your dog. Do not spray directly at their face.

To get around the neck and behind the ears, dampen a soft cloth with the mixture and wipe it on. Lightly spray their bedding and resting areas.

Home-Made Flea Collar

A flea collar is a great way to ward off fleas and is free of all toxins.

Ingredients:

- 3-5 drops of cedar oil or lavender EO
- 1-3 tablespoons of water
- Bandana OR your dog's collar
- Eyedropper (optional)

DIRECTIONS:

Dilute 2-3 drops of your chosen oil in 1-3 tablespoons of water. Apply 5-10 drops of the mixture the bandana or collar and rub the sides of the fabric together. Reapply oil mixture to the collar once a week. In conjunction with this, 1 or 2 drops of oil diluted with at least 1 tablespoon of olive oil can be placed at the base of your dog's tail.

Healthy Cell Growth

For aging dogs, apply these essential oils directly to their spine and paws. This method will boost regeneration of healthy cells and prolong their general wellbeing.

HOW TO:

- Apply 1 drop of Frankincense directly on the spine
- 1 drop of lavender on paws
- 2 times daily

No Bug Zone

HOW TO:

- Surround your pet's food and water bowl with baking soda to keep pests away
- If they are stubborn use 5-10 drops of peppermint essential oils into a box of baking soda and shake to mix. Spread the peppermint baking soda in effected areas.

Paw Balm

When your dog's paws are bothering them, then gentle rub the Paw Balm into the pads of their feet.

HOW TO:
- Add 2 tablespoons of shea butter
- 2 tablespoons of coconut oil
- 1 teaspoon of jojoba oil
- 2 tablespoons of beeswax
- Into a small glass jar
- Place the glass jar into the saucepan and turn on low heat
- Once melted stir oils together well

- Remove the warm glass jar
- Add 2 drops of lavender EO
- 2 drops of frankincense EO to the jar
- Stir well
- Let sit until cool
- Apply to your dog's paws as needed

Pet Tooth Paste

Use baking soda to brush your pets' teeth. It is safe non-toxic and works miracles on plaque.

HOW TO:

- Mix a small amount of baking soda, coconut oil and water to make a paste
- Put the paste on the toothbrush
- Brush gently

FYI: Your pet cannot spit out the extra, so be sure to use a little at a time.

Safe Ant & Spider Spray

My go to ant and spider problem solver, is a classic peppermint spray remedy. This mixture will keep ants and spiders out of your home and yard with absolutely no chemicals or toxins!

Ingredients:
- 1 small spray bottle
- Distilled water
- 2 tablespoons of witch hazel
- 12 drops of peppermint EO

DIRECTIONS:
Take your small spray bottle and fill it 3/4 full of distilled water. Add 2 tablespoons of witch hazel to the spray bottle. Then add 12 drops of Peppermint Essential Oil. Shake it well and spray away!

Victory
Most bugs, especially ants and spiders, despise the smell of peppermint. It doesn't kill them, they just hate it with a passion and stay away at all cost. That is why I am such a huge fan of this remedy. I keep the bugs away and they get to keep their life. It is a win-win for everyone.

Versatile

Spray it around the insides of your doors and windows, or anywhere you believe the critters are getting in. You can also spray a little near the water or food dishes. This is a great spray for the patio, grilling and pool area. Everyone will love the incredible smell of the peppermint.

Ant hills

Place a few drops of Peppermint Essential Oil in the opening of the ant hill and they will hit the road!

Tear Eyes

IT'S NOT YOUR PUPPIES FAULT

Wet tearing eyes are usually a sign of a poor allergen laced diet. Most breeders will have their dogs on diets plum full of allergens. In these cheap food, there are also a plethora of dyes, sugars and strange chemicals causing inflammation.

SUGAR

Sugar is your pooch's worst nightmare. It causes and or allows fungus and yeast to grow ramped. If something is moist and smells funny anywhere on your dog, then you have a sugar problem.

BAD WATER

Tear staining may be further compounded by bad water. If the water has a high mineral content it is more likely to cause stains. You can try demineralized house water, or better yet used a purified water source.

TEETHING

Puppies tend to have worse tear staining when they are teething. Since this is a temporary stage it will lesson within time.

ENVIRONMENT

Tear stains can also be worsened by a dusty or smoky environment.

DOCTORED PHOTOS

It is very normal for our little puppies to have eye stains. For those who are purchasing (or have) purchased online, many times breeders will touch up the photos so that we cannot see the obvious. For those who have, or will see the puppy prior to purchasing, a really good bath and eye stain wash can also fool you.

SOLUTIONS

Either way I wouldn't stress about it. There are plenty of natural tear stain solutions and cleaners in every pet store or online. Make sure that you are paying special attention to their diet and the problem should solve itself without any extra help. If you are going to use a tear stain remover or medication, find a non-toxic formula that uses nature instead of laboratory chemicals.

Getting Rid of Tear Eyes

If you have corrected your dog's diet, and there is still a small amount of tear stain residue, I have a few helpful tricks.

PUPPY CUT FOR ALL AGES
Keep the hair to the inside of the eye super short and the snout hair slightly longer. This will ensure the eye hair doesn't goop up and cause more agitation. The fluffy snout hair will offer a layer of coverage to the stained area.

DAMP MOIST RAG
Every morning gently wipe down the eye area to remove the colored liquid. In addition, if you press gently underneath the inside corner of their eye in an upward motion you will unclog the tear ducks.

BATH YOUR POOCH WEEKLY
Use an all-natural wash that only has a few ingredients. This wash will not irritate your doggies skin and can be used weekly if desired.

Upset Stomach

If you dog is suffering from an upset stomach then help them out with this remedy. Your pooch may be vomiting, refusing food or trying to eat your lawn.

How To:

- Mix 3 drops of tarragon EO
- 2 drops of peppermint EO
- 1 tablespoon of jojoba oil
- Into a glass jar or roller.
- rub a small amount gently on their belly

Waterless Dog Bath

Dry clean your dog! It works the same as dry shampoo for humans.

HOW TO:

- Just sprinkle your pooch with baking soda
- Massage it in
- Brush it out
- It's completely non-toxic and safe for your furry friend

Wipe Out Worms

These are completely safe and non-toxic solution for deworming your dog.

Conventional wormers are chemical-based pesticides, containing carcinogens and toxins that are harmful. These chemicals build up in your doggy's system over time, causing internal damage. Fortunately, there are so many natural ways to remove worms.

Worms are everywhere

Many pet owners have a misconception that dogs either have worms or they don't. While this could be true at any given moment, dogs come in contact with worms on a fairly regular basis. Most worms die before becoming an issue, if your pooch's immune system is running at optimal speed.

With that being said, worms should be viewed as something that must be managed constantly through diet and preventive measures.

Caring Cures for Deworming

I have provided a very useful list of local whole foods that can be administered on a regular basis to prevent and manage worms.

Although I am focusing on our pets, these foods are also wonderful for our own management of parasites. Use the following remedies below on a daily basis if you know your pooch has a worm infestation. If not, then try incorporating them into their diet weekly for optimal worm prevention.

PUMPKIN SEEDS

These tasty snacks are the most potent and effective curative agent against tapeworm and hookworm. Scientific studies have shown that pumpkin seed elements are effective in eliminating these worms in both human and animals. Cucurbitacin, an amino acid in the pumpkin seed eliminates the parasites from the dog's belly and at the same time providing a rich source of zinc, calcium, potassium, niacin and Vitamin A.

How to use:

Use a grinder to grind the raw or sprouted pumpkin seeds into a very fine powder. Mix ½ teaspoon to every 5 pounds of your dog's weight in their food daily. If using as only a preventative measure, try adding to their food one time per week.

CLOVES

Cloves have been by ancient cultures to treat parasites in humans and is often found in anti-parasitic mixtures.

How to use:

Provide ½ of a clove per day for one week for every 5 pound of dog weight. This could be ground and mixed in the food or whole. After this, every other week for the next two months. By then, parasites would have been expelled.

OREGON GRAPE ROOT

The medicinal properties come from the roots of the plant, not the berries. The plant contains berberine a substance that boost the immune system, rids infections and act as an antiseptic. It is effective against viruses, bacteria, fungi and parasites. The plant also is used to cleanse and support the liver.

How to use:

The medicinal properties of Oregon grape are best used by tincture. Three drops to 5 pounds of dog weight, twice per day for one week. Do not medicate pregnant dogs and those with liver problems. Use only if your pooch currently has a worm infestation. Try the other whole food methods listed in this section for prevention.

TURMERIC

This spice has anti-parasitic properties and creates an environment that is not conducive to the growth of worms. Turmeric also heals the areas of the intestines were the worm infestation occurred.

How to use:

Grate 1/8 tsp. per day, for every 5 pounds of dog weight. Make sure your dog has lots of fresh water to ensure that they don't get constipated. Turmeric powder is just fine to use if you cannot find the fresh root. This root looks like ginger but is orange instead. Cut the outside skin off and shred the root over a fine grater.

PAPAYA

Papaya is a great source of digestive enzymes that carries out protein digestion of parasites.

How to use:

Look for a mature green papaya in the nearest food store. Dice fruit into bite sized chunks and add a small amount to your doggy's food. If they digest it well then you can add a little more to their next meal. This is also a great superfood to add to their regular diet.

DIATOMACEOUS EARTH

Diatomaceous earth is a white powdery substance that is made from fossilized remains of small water creatures.

How to use:

Only ensure that you select the one labeled as food grade. Smaller dogs can get one 1/4 of a teaspoon daily. Always mix the substance thoroughly in the dog's meal so they do not inhale it accidently. Use only if your pooch currently has a worm infestation. Try the other whole food methods listed in this section for regular prevention.

CARROTS

Carrots are a safe source of nutrients and great support for your dog's immune system. Also, excellent for using in combination with raw pumpkin seed powder, Oregon grape, turmeric, papaya or clove.

How to use:

Add coarsely chopped carrots to your dog's food. Carrots act as roughage as it goes through the gut. It will scrape all mucus from the walls of the stomach and intestines bringing with it all parasites that are lodged. This is also a great superfood to add to their regular diet.

www.ingramcontent.com/pod-product-compliance
Lightning Source LLC
Chambersburg PA
CBHW060145050426
42448CB00010B/2301